About th

By the time I'd reached my mid-forties I had become really quite good at being me, but then I began to study canine psychology.

A dog whisperer now for the past decade or so, in writing this book, my hope is to share a light with you that found me when I was completely lost, in the darkest place I've ever been to.

THE UNDOING OF EVERYTHING

Bark Eurich

THE UNDOING OF EVERYTHING

Vanguard Press

VANGUARD PAPERBACK

A CIP catalogue record for this title is
available from the British Library.

ISBN 978-1-80016-020-0

*Vanguard Press is an imprint of
Pegasus Elliot MacKenzie Publishers Ltd.*
www.pegasuspublishers.com

First Published in 2021

**Vanguard Press
Sheraton House Castle Park
Cambridge England**

Printed & Bound in Great Britain

Introduction

One day my self-worth, self-esteem and self-belief will despair at who I used to be.
One day fear and anxiety will lose their hold over me.
One day I will embrace who I truly am.
One day I will forget how to say yes when I mean no.
One day I will recognise when I am lying.
One day those lies will stop.
One day I will kick myself for always being strong instead of brave.
One day I will realise that this is my one and only chance of life.
One day I will see that I was not alone in feeling lost.
One day I will see much of what we are taught as a lie.

One day I will wish that I'd known all this as a child.

One day, however
I will step out of the dark
and I'll find myself free,
ready and able to live my own life,
content and soulfully at peace,
just being me.

Chapter One
Friend

noun

A person with whom one has a bond of mutual affection, Typically, one exclusive of sexual or family relations.

The friend, who came into our lives and then went on to change the course of the human being's evolutionary trail, was only made possible at all because of Mother Nature's inability to bend her own rules.

Dogs are the result of man's universal failed attempt to domesticate the Wolf, from the Great Dane to a Chihuahua, whatever breed they happen to be, every Dog's DNA will be almost identical to that of the Grey Wolf.

Without man interfering in the Wolf's own natural breeding selection process, there would likely be no such thing today as a Bulldog a Rottweiler or a Pug.

As hard as it might be to recognise the Wolf in any shape or form when comparing it to a Dog such as a Pug, imagine how equally hard it must be for Dogs to recognise the human beings who first befriended the Wolf all those years ago, in the supposedly now advanced people they see running around today's fast moving plastic world.

Human beings have the largest brains on the planet, but sadly our laziness, our arrogance and our insecurity combined with our modern contempt for nature, have left us forgetting how to use them.

Knowledge, and the lessons of life are things we often pride ourselves on being able to pass on to the next generation, with every parent wanting better or more for their offspring than they managed to have themselves.

Yet, since the dawn of time, everyone, no matter what generation they were born into, has always looked down on the wet behind the ears, waste of space generation following them, even though, each and every one of us can only be the product of the maybe not quite so smart after all generation that actually raised us.

With the aid of this little book, you are about to hear a voice that has largely been ignored by us for the best part of forty thousand years. Quite how this ever happened will probably remain as a benchmark and reminder to humanity for the rest of eternity, of just how stupid the largest brain on the planet can be.

It is in hearing this voice, reconnecting with Nature, and understanding exactly what our closest link with Nature is trying to tell us, about us, today, in this crazy world of ours, that will undoubtedly change your way of thinking forever.

Friend

noun

Someone with whom one has an unbreakable bond built on a foundation of mutual trust and respect whose advice comes without religious, political, commercial or fashionable agenda.

Someone who not only knows you better than you know them, but probably knows you even better than you do too.

A friend that is so in tune with us that they'll know you are pregnant before you do, they'll also know that you're about to have a fit, an attack or a hypo before you do. Knowing that you have cancer long before your doctor could possibly have any idea is, of course, another one of their many party tricks.

But a Dog's ability to save a human from themselves or modern life doesn't come from any kind of supernatural ability of theirs, but rather, it is what Dogs are completely incapable of doing, that can be the game changer for people in the world of human mental wealth.

Unlike us, Dogs cannot lie. We lie so much that we've forgotten what the truth actually looks like, but our simple friends with their little brains are so dumb that they can only tell the truth.

This sometimes inconvenient reality is further compounded by another difference between humans and canines, which is that Dogs cannot rationalise either.

These are the two differences between human and canine psychology that you'll come to recognise as two of the four quarters of a language that are going to do everything they can to make you whole again.

The third quarter of this language is born out of correcting what probably has to be the biggest misconception people today have about dogs, which is when they think that a Dog's love is unconditional. Quite simply, in reality, a Dog's love is anything but unconditional, it never has been unconditional nor will it ever be unconditional. To suggest different is both an insult to Dogs, to love itself and indeed a belittling of the most important relationship we as a species have ever had.

The fourth quarter of this language in a way is a return back to the first quarter, or rather the sting in the first quarter's tail, because not being able to tell a lie themselves, also makes our friends world class lie detectors.

So what does all this mean, lie detectors, Mother Nature and the four quarters of a new language? How does this gobbledegook tie together and turn tangled words from a book, into tangible, life changing, practical and cognitive life tools, for you?

The first simple steps on this majestic journey begin to unfold naturally when ensuring that trust, respect and communication between our two species are once again genuine two-way streets.

People often equate their love of Dogs as the same thing as being good with Dogs.

However, in the same way that loving food doesn't automatically make anyone a good cook, what makes somebody good with Dogs will have very little to do with their own capacity to love them.

A Dog's ability to love you isn't necessarily going to mirror how much you love them either, but rather their displays of affection and loyalty will be a direct reflection of how much that Dog actually trusts and respects you.

The modern day problem is that Dogs are very unlikely to have done much of either of those two things if all you yourself have ever done in that relationship, is love them unconditionally, whilst only ever trying to be their friend.

Our journey into the mind of Dogs, if not already confusing enough, must sadly begin with something of a paradox.

Although Dogs are more than happy to hammer home life lessons that will no doubt often feel quite if not completely counter-intuitive to you, in the interests of harmonious human-canine relationships, this particular little nugget is, not to put too fine a point on it, rather a big deal.

It's the backbone of this book and probably the one thing that seems to trip most people up when they're trying to establish a meaningful relationship with a Dog.

The sentiment of this, is the reason behind most of the unwanted behaviour issues that Dogs often give their owners, and for good measure, it also happens to be one of the two main influences behind why more than six hundred people in Great Britain are bitten or attacked by Dogs, every single day.

So, without further ado, welcome to the world of rehabilitation by canine, my friend. Your likely long overdue wakeup call and a big fat reality check awaits.

This journey can be something of an emotional roller coaster, as truth from our best friends is always instant and can at times be a bit brutal.

So even though I'm asking you to prepare for what might, emotionally at least, end up being a bit of a bumpy ride, please do so knowing that your opponent in this particular battle, is someone who wholeheartedly wants you to win.

Chapter Two
Lie Detectors

The animal that had already sensed your out of control and escalating heart rate, long before you yourself had realised that you were having a full blown panic attack, happens to be the same animal that knew your blood sugar levels had dropped through the floor, long before your hypo actually had you on the floor.

With their incredible senses, Dogs are constantly and acutely aware of exactly what kind of a day we're having, even if we ourselves at the time happen to be so wrapped up in our day, that we hadn't yet realised what effects our day was actually having on us.

On the positive side, their uncanny ability to constantly and very accurately read our state of mind, is ultimately what gives Dogs the power to change a person's life.

Sadly though, underestimating the significance of this ability of theirs, leads to one of the most common mistakes people make when they are around Dogs, which is that they don't fully appreciate just how much their own state of mind influences the behaviour of their Dog.

If walking your Dog feels more like hanging on to

the back of a runaway train, if you know deep down that without that sack of treats in your cupboard your Dog would otherwise ignore you, or if your Dog's recall is more throwing a stick than a boomerang, then your very own agenda-free lie detector will no doubt have one or two rather important things that they have been trying to say to you.

The crazy thing is, that instead of continually having your arm pulled out of its socket, once you are able to have that very same Dog walk beautifully by your side, when their recall is like having a Dog on a long piece of elastic, and when you've given up needing to buy their loyalty with endless bags of treats, that Dog will be seeing you in a very different light to how they're used to seeing you.

When this happens, Dogs won't be the only ones noticing big changes in you.

Because of its significance, the lie detector explanation comes in three parts, any of these topics by themselves are quite benign, with no one subject being more important than another, but the culmination of all three of them working together at the same time, quickly becomes a stone in the shoe for any Dog owner intent on walking down a path of denial, delusion or even self-destruction.

Lie Detectors Part One
Tell Tails

Imagine for a minute that you are reading this book sat by a window in a busy high street café. Whilst you're sat there getting your caffeine fix, you happen to look through the window out across the bustling street and notice two men stood waiting at a bus stop, both talking on their phones.

Unbeknown to you. one of them had been making funeral arrangements for the daughter he just lost in a tragic road accident, the other guy had just been told that he's won the lottery.

Without being able to hear a single word of their conversation, but instead only relying on what you had seen, you would still have a pretty good idea of which one of those men was having a good day and which of them wasn't.

Every emotion that a Dog experiences will be physically expressed instantaneously in some way through their body, and as their primary means of communicating with each other, Dogs are absolute masters at reading one another's body language.

Tails hanging down still like a wet length of rope, waving around uncontrollably, wedged firmly between their legs or even stuck up in the air rigid like a flagpole, all give us a clear insight into what's actually going on between that Dog's ears.

So does in fact, the very position of those ears,

whether they are assertively held forward, curiously sticking up, out to the sides or submissively held close down by the neck — all have their own very significant meanings.

The softness or intensity of their eyes, the posturing, the arch or straightness of the back, how they move and hold themselves, how high or low they hold their head as they approach you, curled lip, sideways glances, hackles, and whether they want to smell you or not.

A fluid, real time and silent language, that leaves every Dog knowing exactly where they stand with every other Dog around them, every second, of every day.

Something that often catches people out when attempting to enjoy or establish a meaningful relationship with a Dog, is that as good as Dogs are at reading each other, as you might expect, they're also red hot at reading our body language too.

Within the first few seconds of a Dog meeting you, that Dog will have already established for themselves exactly what kind of a person they see you as, and by that time, the ground rules will have already been laid for what kind of a relationship you can then expect to go on and enjoy, or indeed endure, with that particular Dog.

Lie Detectors Part Two
Cards on the Table

A Dog's razor-sharp ability to notice when you're not in good shape is far from being restricted to the role of a Medical Detection Dog.

There is no question that the use of Dogs within modern medicine will continue to be an expanding field, and will become more and more familiar to us all.

Your GP, for example, will only have about five million receptors in their nose, meaning that just like the rest of us, they don't have the ability to smell things like cancer on your breath.

Unlike the nose of a German Shepherd or a Rottweiler, who have the best part of quarter of a billion receptors in their noses, and can indeed detect cancer on somebody's breath.

With almost half of us now expected to contract cancer in some form or another during our lifetime, maybe the receptionist at your local doctor's surgery always should have been a Rottweiler after all?

A Dog's intuitive detection capabilities are as valuable to us as they are incredible, but the reason canine psychology and protocol should be taught in all schools throughout Britain, quickly becomes apparent once our closest link with Mother Nature becomes your life coach.

There are only two reasons why anybody would ever have to experience behavioural problems with a

Dog: ignorance and confidence.

Things like bad recall, anti-social issues, aggression problems or just impossible to walk on a lead, all stem from the same two places, neither of which have much to do with Dogs at all: ignorance and confidence, yours.

The truth is the only reason a Dog will continue trying to pull your arm out of its socket as you attempt to walk them on a lead, is because you keep telling that Dog that you're very happy for them to be doing so, otherwise, in their mind at least, why would you keep doing it, or more to the point, why on Earth would you keep allowing it, especially when you don't have to?

Not knowing how or what to do when a relationship with a Dog is going wrong, will inevitably make anybody less confident in anything that they are actually trying to do.

Which is then always going to leave the door wide open for frustration, anxiety and even fear to join you and your Dog on your walk, which, by the way, just happen to be the three things that will almost certainly prevent you from ever having either a healthy relationship with or indeed of ever having any real control over that Dog.

If you are determined to only ever see your Dog as your baby, a teddy bear or a surrogate child, it is unlikely that Dog will ever be much of a life coach for you.

The same must also be said for anyone making

what is another very common but still quite detrimental mistake.

As cold or distant as this may initially sound to a Dog lover, in the interests of you having a balanced, respectful, harmonious, stress free relationship with a Dog, it is always worth remembering that the last thing your Dog will ever want to see you as, is their friend.

To understand exactly why this is, you only have to spend time watching Dogs interacting with one another within a pack.

When everything is happy everyone is happy, but the bottom line is that in times of great stress, excitement, danger or confusion, Dogs are unlikely to listen to their friends or look to them for direction or advice.

If a Dog sees another as nothing more than an equal, or less, to them, they'll have no reason whatsoever to respect them, and without respect, so called friendship can all of a sudden turn into full on rivalry.

The same Dogs that are more than happy to all squeeze on the same sofa together are very unlikely to be as quick to share their bone or indeed their food with anyone. Feeding time with a pack of Dogs is when anyone is most likely to realise just how important it is that Dogs respect you first, long before they love you or see you as an equal.

Without one single exception, every Dog will wholeheartedly rejoice inside when they're forced into taking up the life coach role for their owner, and really you only have to look at the positive benefits that then come their way to understand exactly why.

I mean, imagine how you yourself would feel if suddenly a big fat rock landed smack bang in the middle of your life, who then refused to allow you to be afraid anymore, a calming influence who'd never let your anxiety run away with you.

Someone who recognised and respected you for who you really are, who would never lead you into trouble, whose only agenda was to see you soulfully happy, but would also bite your arse every time you said yes when you really meant to say no.

In part three of lie detectors the pack are going to start asking you what might end up being some pretty tough questions about what sort of a person you are.

The problem is that you won't consciously get a chance to answer these important questions yourself, because with Dogs being Dogs, they will already know the answers.

To better prepare yourself for what happens when your ignorance and your lack of confidence start knocking seven shades out of each other, we have to look into the future, and see where you'll finally end up when your *One Day* has at last become your every day.

The bottom line or conclusion to having been rehabilitated by canines, is simply nothing more than you are going to enjoy the ability to live in complete harmony with any Dog at any time anywhere in the world.

By this time, two-way streets of understanding, trust, respect and communication with an animal will have become second nature to you. However, what might not be quite so second nature to you anymore, is being who you used to be or acting the way you used to allow yourself to act, before you stepped up and became everything to someone, who by the way, now absolutely adores you.

Training Dogs with the use of Dog treats is all very well, as long as you take these four factors into due consideration;

One, over the past decade, Britain's canine community's consumption, or use of Dog treats nationwide has gone up by a massive 73%, but over this same period of time, the number of people being hospitalised due to Dog attacks has risen by 87%.

Two, it is impossible to train a Dog to respect you, because they either do or they don't, and if they don't respect you, it will be your fault not theirs.

Three, what do you become to your Dog when you run out of treats?

Four, the next time you stand in front of a mirror, take a really good look at what your Dog's treat should actually look like.

The differences between the person that deep down is the real you, and the person that you might have allowed yourself to become over the course of your life, will be identified the moment you acknowledge and respect the ground rules that all members of the pack live and die by.

Rules which always come down from the top, and were already successfully in play thirty thousand years before the Neolithic even thought about building Stonehenge.

The first of these rules conveniently introduces us to the third part of my lie detectors explanation, because in you setting out to become somebody that Dogs will naturally and wilfully want to respect, it is vital to remember that as unlikely as they are to ever listen to their friends, the one thing that Dogs are absolutely guaranteed never to listen to, is crazy.

Lie Detectors Part Three
Larkin' About

If you thought making a Dog respect you, has anything to do with making sure that Dog fears you, then please think very carefully again.

If a Dog fears you they're unlikely ever to completely trust you, and if they don't trust you, you'll have even less chance of successfully winning over their hearts and minds than if they only had contempt for you.

If our chief executive officer, our local MP or indeed our Prime Minister are seen by us all as weak, directionless, corrupt, not respecting us or just not taking us where we want to go, their term in office will be short lived.

Every captain has his sergeant, every sergeant has his corporals, every corporal his lance corporal, and all for very good reason.

Leadership for the human being is very important and structures our day to day, but in times of crisis good leadership becomes essential.

It may take weeks to crown a new monarch, days to replace a prime minister, but on the battlefield, that sergeant becomes a captain, the very second his captain is no longer there.

Dogs are of course, no different to us in their need for stability, so it is crucial to understand that within every pack of Dogs there will always be somebody at the top, a top Dog, their pack leader or the alpha.

Whatever title you wish to give them, the guys at the top of the tree are the ones we really need to pay most attention to, because these are the guys who will give you all the clues you need, on how to become the best thing that could ever happen to your Dog.

Just like humans, few Dogs are actually natural born leaders. Most are not interested in the huge responsibility of taking up the alpha role at all, much preferring instead to simply follow, and support somebody they're happy to trust and respect.

However, if Dogs suddenly find themselves with no leadership at all, they're all hard wired to then take up the vacant leadership role themselves, and that is something you, as that Dog's owner, never want to allow to happen, ever.

As that Dog's owner, you yourself really don't want that unsettling feeling of being led anywhere by an unbalanced nervous stress head who can't handle responsibility, who is effectively afraid of their own shadow or just panics and goes into an emotional meltdown in the face of something new or unfamiliar to them, do you?

No?

Good, because neither does your Dog.

In the poem *This be the verse*, the poet Philip Larkin suggests that however much they may have loved you, and however unintentional the consequences of their actions may have been, the reality is that through their own fears, their own inadequacies or insecurities, in some way or another, your parents will inevitably 'fuck you up'.

Quite how much Mr Larkin's suggestion weighs on you personally, will depend on nothing more than who your parents happened to be, but your childhood family home is far from being the only place where people get to learn how to be crazy.

Sibling rivalry, peer pressure, society's expectations, jealous and controlling partners, failed business ventures, bereavement, job loss, stress related illness, counsellors who only ever ask you what you think, and GPs now readily acting like pimps for the big pharmaceutical drug companies.

We can all line up the people in our life that have

hurt us, and there are indeed an infinite number of reasons how a baby born pure into this world, can end up as an adult with a catalogue of genuine bona fide and defendable reasons for acting like a complete idiot.

The trouble is, or rather, the fantastic, life changing, head clearing, and empowering thing, for you, is that not one of those out of date and overused detrimental excuses of yours will ever mean a thing to your Dog.

This is where our friends play their sledgehammer of a trump card, which is the second of the four quarters of the language that is going to make you whole again.

Dogs cannot rationalise, so, whatever those acute senses of theirs are telling them about you, is not only absolutely how that Dog sees you, but absolutely how you are.

Take anger, for example. As with any emotion, it won't matter exactly what you have allowed to upset you or why you are carrying on being angry around your Dog, because all that will be evident and indeed all that will matter to that Dog, at that time, is that you are angry.

Which means that as a Dog owner, you will then be suffering an added punishment to those people who are just angry but don't have a Dog, because all the time you are happy to continue acting like an angry idiot, your status, in the eyes of your Dog at least, will steadily, and rightfully, become nothing.

In conclusion to lie detectors, our best friend is an animal that demands we act and be a certain way around them, in order for them to be able to trust and respect us enough for them to then willingly give us their hearts and minds.

If however we fail to conform to their demands, and don't act and be that certain way for them, we can quickly start to lose their respect and their ability to trust us, and at the same time we then wave goodbye to any real chance we ever had of that Dog seeing us as the best thing that has ever happened to them.

We also know that Dogs are so tapped into us that they'll often be more aware of our actual state of mind than even we might be ourselves, at the time.

So, every time you lose your head, the reality is that you'll have already lost your Dog too, and with you now not wanting to lose your Dog, it means that you, that Dog's owner, might have to start being a little more accountable for how you allow yourself to act, and react, to certain situations when you are around your Dog.

Failing to convince a Dog that you are no longer crazy is when you'll see the full force of their lie detecting skills come into play.

After all, the only way you'll ever convince a Dog that you are not angry, is if you're not angry, and if deep down you are still angry, they'll know, and they'll have no problem reacting to your anger accordingly.

On your path to gaining hero status with your Dog, you might have to change a thing or two about your behaviour and how you allow yourself to be, how long you want to hang on to things like anger and frustration, and how much you want that to keep on affecting your day versus how much of a canine hero you want to be.

Maybe you've never had somebody constantly in your face and on your case demanding that you keep yourself together, or maybe you've never actually had anyone in your life who genuinely cared how crazy you got or what state of mind you've let yourself get into. But make no mistake, with a Dog in your life, right now you most definitely do have that somebody.

Chapter Three
Mindset

Whether you were a human baby or a canine puppy, by the time you have reached adulthood, the people who raised you will have had a huge impact on who you are, how you think and act, and how you see both yourself and the rest of the world.

None of us get to choose our childhood or have any say in what kind of people our parents might be, in much the same way that a young Pup has little choice as to how much of a lunatic their new owner will turn out to be.

The wonderful thing about being messed up by your supposedly messed up parents, however, is that once you yourself have taken the time to look at the world through your own eyes, used the brain that you were born with, listened to your own heart and grown a spine, you'll realise that at no time has it ever been mandatory for you to spend your whole life upholding every single family tradition.

In the last chapter I used anger as one example of an emotion that Dogs are very likely to have a problem with, and that in itself is the reason why you'll find canine heroes do their best to make sure that they keep a lid on their anger.

You may well come from a family of angry, non-communicative, stressed out door slammers, but, whenever you have a Dog lead in your hand, you automatically, and immediately, become the most important person in the world to somebody who is also rather important to you.

To keep portraying yourself as an unbalanced angry idiot to your life coach is, of course, a great way to find yourself once again sliding quickly back down the scale from hero to zero.

So, if you are someone who really wants to become a canine hero, but you still have a habit of forgetting that the punishment for being constantly angry, is being constantly angry, your best mate is now in your life to constantly remind you.

This is the point when any wannabe a canine hero is going to find themselves having to make a potentially life changing choice.

Either they continue allowing themselves to lose their head all the time and therefore continue losing their Dog, all the time or they start putting a lot of stuff that obviously doesn't belong to them down, allowing them to then to step up, and rightfully become somebody's hero.

As counter intuitive or even annoying as those terms and conditions might seem, this dilemma can end up being a very simple life choice for an animal lover to make, only because sometimes there can be no sweeter choice for us, than when we have absolutely no choice at all.

However, if you are the sort of person that actually enjoys being angry, and the very thought of you having to give up your right to act like an unbalanced idiot is already giving you the wobbles, then please don't panic, you will still have plenty of opportunity in your life to carry on with your old self-destructive ways.

After all, you are not going to be with your beady-eyed life coach twenty-four-seven, I mean, if you leave your Dog at home when you go to work, you'll have all day to carry on being as angry as you like.

At the end of your day there's always your commute too, so if by that time you still haven't been angry enough yet that day, fill your boots on your way home with red mist and plenty of road rage, run people off the road, curse, shout and make lots of vulgar hand gestures at people, even get into fist fights if that really is your thing.

Just as long as you remember that when you do eventually arrive home, before you so much as put your key anywhere near that lock of your front door, make sure your hot little head has cooled down enough to recognise that there's going to be a lie detector on the other side of that door, who'll be eager to find out exactly how their wannabe canine hero is coping with their day.

It may initially be quite difficult for a hot head to fit this particular way of forcing themselves to be more accountable for their behaviour, into their life, but the benefits for anyone who suffers with anger issues will be brought into ever sharper focus once that person becomes intent on having their Dog genuinely adore them.

Old Dogs are never too old to learn new tricks, especially tricks that lead them to enjoying a more balanced, peaceful and rewarding way of being.

Any delays in a Dog learning these new tricks will be down to just how serious their teacher was about being a hero.

The more time a devout hot head spends having to respect the ways and values of their life coach, the less time they'll be left with to spend being angry.

As nobody actually enjoys being angry or gains anything worth having when anger has the better of them, making sure that their best mate continues to see them as a hero, will undoubtedly open the door just enough to see and experience the possibilities of walking a very different path.

Anger is, of course, far from being the only emotion people let get the better of them. However, it is also a very long way from being the only emotion a Dog is going to react badly to should their hero start experiencing too much of it.

The difference between a highly trained Medical Detection Dog, and the average domestic pet, probably best explains how all Dogs are capable of helping to give people their lives back, and also demonstrates why it is so important that a wannabe canine hero learns how to keep a lid on being crazy.

The ability to notice that your imagination has now got the better of you, that your heart rate and breathing patterns are spiralling out of control, and that you are not focused here anymore but instead lost in a world of what might be, is not unique to Medical Detection Dogs.

Trained or not, the fact that you are about to have yet another full blown panic attack will have already been picked up by any Dog, and almost certainly long before you yourself had realised where you were going.

The difference between the Medical Dog and your pet however, is in exactly how each of them react to you being in trouble.

When the Medical Dog realises that you've lost it, they'll be doing everything they can to make sure that your focus then comes away from where you were going straight back on to them, your Dog, and the here and now, demanding you make eye contact with the unbiased face of reality that happens to be staring right back at you.

That Dogs simple, but well-earned and gratefully received reward for doing their job is paid in full, the very moment they get their hero back.

The love for and understanding of that Dog combined with a recognition of exactly what the Dog was actually trying to tell their owner, can be enough of a life tool for somebody to then have the ability to disarm those debilitating attacks in their tracks, even to the point of gradually making them become a thing of their past.

Meanwhile, your average Dog that has had no medical training whatsoever, won't have a clue that you going into meltdown was actually their cue for them to start doing their job, of rescuing you.

However, the problem that you will then be left with is that they still would have recognised that you were in meltdown.

Without that detection training, what else is a Dog then meant to do but tap into their own forty thousand year old instincts.

Meaning that rather than just being a cue for them to go to work, you losing it instead then becomes a cue for them to go about bringing a whole array of different unwanted canine behaviour issues to the table, few of which are likely to be of much help to anyone in trouble, at all.

If anxiety is constantly disrupting your life or fear keeps cropping up and ruining your day. If you're an over wound stress-head, caught up in a hamster wheel, or your self-worth is skulking around somewhere on the floor, it is worth knowing that your Dog won't need to be a qualified and certificated Medical Detection Dog to be able to immediately start helping you bring about positive and empowering changes to your life.

Initially, the only disadvantage you'll have to suffer with a regular Dog over that of a professionally trained Medical Detection Dog, is that you yourself will be the one having to do all the learning, not your Dog.

Instead of a Dog, having to be trained to first ignore their own instincts and then, secondly, communicate with humans in a way humans understand, all that really has to happen when done this way around, is you get a chance to reconnect with nature, as you learn how to read a Dog.

Without exception, when a Dog's owner suddenly finds themselves in a bad place, that Dog will know, and will then react accordingly, no doubt in a very similar way to how most of the other ten million Dogs throughout Britain might also have reacted.

Having a genuine and fundamental understanding of how the minds of Dogs really work, who they'll listen to and who they won't, and why they won't, is going to give anyone a much better chance of having the ability to keep their life coach calm, respectful and under control at all times.

The big bonus coming to anyone who felt they might have been at a disadvantage because they got stuck with their own bog-standard domestic mutt rather than having the privilege of a proper fully trained Medical Detection Dog, is that you'll find the life tools that Mother Nature will have given you on this particular journey, will give you the confidence and the ability to take control of a lot more things in your life than just your Dog.

Chapter Four
Love

Your journey into the canine mind is going to be abrupt and quite bumpy if you try hanging on to the delusion of a Dog's love being in any way unconditional.

There is no such thing as unconditional love, either in the canine world or in ours. Sure, you might claim that you'll love your child (who could later in life turn out to be a serial killer) with all your heart no matter what, but then the very fact that they are your child surely has to be something of a rather big, fat, overwhelmingly important condition all by itself?

However, no matter what, your Dog is definitely not a blood relative of yours in any way, so any actual bond that you do share together will have been earned, by you, being the sort of person, a Dog is naturally going to want to look up to.

A relationship based on tolerating, enduring, putting up with, taking the mick or just making the most of your only option in life are all very different ways of being to that of being adored. The flip-side to this is, that if a Dog does genuinely adore you, it won't be because they didn't have a choice.

Love, believe it or not, is another emotion that can

easily tip the scales and trip us up if we don't watch what we do with it, and getting this bit wrong can very quickly turn a potentially beautiful relationship with a canine into something of a nightmare.

No, this isn't where I'm about to tell you that it's wrong to love a Dog, in fact far from it, but I must make it clear that you giving your love, affection or reward to a Dog, at the wrong time, is one of the quickest ways to destroy any chance you ever had of becoming a canine hero.

It is important to remember that a Dog cannot rationalise, so giving a reward to a Dog is a clear way for them to understand that you are endorsing that Dog's current behaviour, a way of you saying well done, thank you or please carry on, or do that again, for something that they have just done or are currently doing.

However, it is critical to remember that there are two occasions when you should never give your Dog any form of reward or affection.

The first is simply when they don't deserve it, because this will then confuse the hell out of a Dog and make life impossible, I mean if you were dumb enough to reward your Dog by feeding them a nice fat juicy steak just after you found them chewing up one of your shoes, you'll be walking around barefoot for the rest of that Dog's life.

The second occasion is probably a more commonly made mistake and therefore more likely to happen, and sadly, the consequences for the Dog when this does happen can be psychologically catastrophic.

If you yourself are secretly a bit of a big softy when it comes to Dogs, then what I'm about to ask of you will almost certainly go against your kind, nurturing and compassionate nature.

However, bear with me on this particularly crucial point because I'm absolutely not asking anyone to be cold or distant to their Dog, nor am I suggesting that anybody love their Dog less in any way.

In the very same way that it makes absolutely no sense to reward a Dog with affection if that Dog has just been misbehaving for you, if you really want to ramp things up and completely Phillip Larkin a Dog up, then go right ahead and dowse your loving affection all over your cute fur baby whenever the poor little thing shows any sign of distress.

The affection that you share with your Dog should only ever be given by you as a reward and must be associated purely as a positive experience for both you and your Dog. But, those very same loving displays of physical affection should never be used as a way of giving comfort or reassurance to a stressed, hurt or fearful animal.

Physically giving affection to a Dog when they are emotionally in a bad place is never a good idea for either you or your Dog, only because doing this is a fantastically efficient way to quickly achieve the absolute opposite of what you intended.

At the very time a Dog is stressed, confused,

anxious or full of fear, they won't thank you one little bit for any of the comforting affection that you keep trying to give them. After all, why exactly would a canine hero want to endorse or promote their unbalanced or fearful state of mind? What possible reason could you as that Dog's owner have for wanting to reward a Dog for acting like an idiot?

Bed covers, fridge magnets, tea towels, post cards, biscuit tins, cushion covers, even T-shirts, smothered in an old and familiar phrase that we all say but don't always do, *Keep Calm and Carry On*.

Before you get to wear your canine hero T-shirt, you are going to have to pay a lot more than just lip service to this old saying.

A white blinding flash out of the darkness instantly followed by a foundation shaking bang, has just woken you up and made you aware that Mother Nature, despite her inconvenient timing, has parked a thunderstorm with intent right above your house.

This is followed a few seconds later, by the noise of your child, almost taking the door off its hinges as they run into your bedroom like a bat out of hell, intent on finding you.

However much the lightning might be unsettling you yourself, the very fact that you are there for your child, with your hug and continuous back rub will, of course, soon help their fear of the nightmare storm subside.

On top of this we can also rationalise with a child,

so whilst we give them security in our physical hug we can also reassure them by rationalisation, explaining what is actually going on, divert their attention away from the storm by stunning them with science, and if that doesn't work, you can always lie through your back teeth to them.

A wonderful thing about kids is that they are hard wired to believe adults, which makes them as gullible as hell and wide open to be convinced of absolutely anything we tell them. Isn't that right, Mr Larkin?

Once a young child understands that you yourself have been struck by lightning quite a few times in your life and not once had it ever really hurt, and that lightning storms happen because it's the only time Mother Nature gets to make fairy palaces, along with their new found scientifically backed knowledge that every second between a lightning flash and the bang represents a thousand miles, as loud as it still might be, they'll know that they are in fact miles and miles and miles and miles away from any danger.

Unlike your young Pup who is downstairs hiding under the kitchen table, and as this is also their first thunder storm, they are understandably confused and has now become quite anxious.

As you walk into the kitchen you can't help but notice your Pup's quite pathetic body language. Shaking, ears hanging down to the side of their head as if they're made of lead, sullen eyes, head held low with their back arched to almost cowering, tail firmly up between their legs.

Nobody wants to see an animal in distress and yes, of course, it is our natural instinct to give reassuring affection to someone in times of stress, but as Pups are little Dogs and not little people, a keep calm and carry on, canine hero would do no such thing, in fact they'll probably just ignore the Dog.

Even if they came out from under the table and made their own way over to you for reassurance, they'd still probably just ignore the Dog.

But this doesn't mean that the Pup isn't then beginning to get all the reassurance they need.

The golden rule is that if you want to make a big deal out of something, then your Dog will probably be more than happy to oblige.

Okay, big softy, I know all you really want to do is pick that cute and still afraid Puppy up to reassure them with a hug, like you were just able to do for your child only moments ago. The trouble is your Pup's not a child and by the way, that Puppy is also still full of anxiety.

So, canine hero, let's start thinking like a Dog and help our Pup instead of letting a guilt ridden or over sentimental human imagination turn a healthy Dog into a nut case.

It goes without saying that in reality nobody is actually ignoring anybody. We are fully aware that our little friend is stressed out at the moment, and that is exactly why they'll not be getting any fuss from us, yet.

As you sit there at the table you may not be

physically interacting with them, but, the message you are giving out will be quite clear and also very welcome to them.

The person they now look up to the most in the world, the one they look to for guidance and leadership, and the one wanting to be known as a canine hero, isn't reacting badly to those unfamiliar loud bangs from outside. In fact, their keep calm and carry on hero is simply just keeping calm and carrying on as if nothing was wrong.

The longer that Pup then spends around somebody who isn't panicking or afraid, who is instead just enjoying the light show and spending some time with their Pup, the sooner that Pup is going to realise that there never was a problem, that their initial fears were unfounded, and then they'll start to relax.

The ears will liven up, the back will start to loosen up and straighten, their nose might even come into play as fear turns to curiosity and the tail will then finally come out from between their legs.

Now, my compassionate, big softy friends, that tail coming out from between their legs was what you have been waiting for, that was your green light to finally go help yourself and give that Pup all the affection you want.

Whilst you are doing so, congratulate yourself on a job well done. Your patience and alpha attitude both prevented the birth of a potentially problematic behaviour issue dead in its tracks and also laid the foundations for a bond with an animal built on nothing more than trust and genuine adoration.

However guilty or bad you might have felt when you were initially ignoring your Pup, understand that there is absolutely nothing cold or distant about refusing to allow fear or anxiety to run away with your best friend's life.

Chapter Four
Attitude and Accountability

How much you either enjoy or fear lightning will have played a huge part in just how successful you would have been at helping your Pup through their first experience of a thunderstorm.

If you were just hopelessly pretending to be calm, but in reality you were actually worried senseless, your little lie detector would have already known, and because of this, then wouldn't have been able to calm down one little bit, and so today would no doubt still have issues even at the very sound of an approaching storm, plus you wouldn't have had the chance to earn all those Brownie points the way you did.

In somebody's eyes you are the most important human being in the world, so imagine how good your life coach is going to start feeling about themselves whenever they are in your company, with you now there steadfast as their hero, to fight their corner.

Not allowed to be scared anymore, not allowed to get too anxious, not allowed to get too angry, not allowed to get too aggressive, not allowed to get too stressed or too excited, actually not allowed to get too anything anymore.

Never allowed to obsess, not allowed to feel bad about yourself, not allowed to get too emotional, not allowed to let your imagination take you to places that don't exist, not allowed to say yes when you really meant no, not allowed to act like a victim, not allowed to be a doormat and therefore no longer allowed to forget who you really are.

A timid wallflower that nobody ever sees through to the arrogant arse who makes sure everyone sees them, whomever or whatever you have become, the benefits that you'll experience when you make sure that your Pup has every reason to always see you as a hero, doesn't mean that you'll not be able to be you anymore, it only means that you'll no longer be allowed to be the stupid, low self-esteem, stressed-out, clock-watching, over-excitable, unbalanced, twenty-first century idiot version of you.

Taking the alpha role for the sake of your Pup's welfare, demanding things are right and making sure that your life goes your way, instead of just sitting back watching and hoping everything turns out nice for you, means that whilst you are in the company of your Dog at least, you'll really have no choice but to become the true, untainted, confident and soulfully at peace person that you were born to be, and would always have been, had you not allowed life to keep on biting you.

For a lot of people the very thought of having to take up the alpha role in any way, at all, let alone demand things like respect from a cute, fluffy and adorable young Pup, will likely go completely against their own nature.

But if you yourself can't imagine ever demanding anything from anybody, the chances are that your little life coach will have come into your life for a very good reason.

For some of us the thought of having to change our ways can be as scary as hell, even if we know that not changing means we'll only guarantee the continuation of the actual hell that we're already subjecting ourselves to on a daily basis.

So, if you are indeed somebody who is still allowing life to constantly bite you, you should understand that in choosing to take the alpha role, if only for the sake of your Dog, willing or not, you'll experience the full power and beauty of Mother Nature's wisdom at work, and this is where you end up with the emotional tool kit capable of making all the biting stop.

Cars do not get their owners speeding tickets or parking fines. The most dangerous thing about any motorbike is the nut holding the handlebars. Never in mankind's history has a gun ever shot anybody, knives do not stab people and Dogs do not give their owners behaviour issues.

Doormats, however, do still get walked on.

Loving a Pup with unearned or unjustified affection, becoming their best friend and forgetting all about the rules for creating a harmonious and respectful human canine relationship is the easiest thing in the world to do.

With a young Pup only weighing a few kilos and being no real danger to anyone but themselves, you might argue that there's no need or even room for such things as discipline and respect in a canine kindergarten.

Even though that Pup's mother herself, would have unashamedly and instantly demanded respect and instilled discipline in that Pup, for her sake, for the sake of all her other Pups, and indeed for that pup's sake, from the very moment that Pup was born.

The thing is, having a Puppy that hasn't learnt how to respect you yet, that never really listens to you or only gives you the run around, is one thing, but within a year those few kilos can end up being forty kilos or more.

At twelve months old Dogs are already sexually mature and will be somewhere close to the size they'll be as a full blown adult, not unlike a fifteen year old human.

So, if all you have ever done through their entire life is try to be their friend, having them see you as their equal and then subsequently spend your whole life quietly worrying about whether they love you or not.

Instead of just getting on with being the best version of you that you could be, by quietly making sure that you were the one person in their world that they'd willingly look up to and respect.

If, in fact, proper communications, understanding and respect for one another have never truly been established, for all your hard work, hopes, sleepless nights and best wishes, the relationship that you now enjoy with that fifteen-year-old human being, is unlikely to be the most rewarding thing that you've ever done in your life, for you.

The bad news is that on a day-to-day basis there will be no let up for you with a lie detecting, hyper-alert, always on your case, canine life coach either. However, our super sensitive friends do have a rather beautiful saving grace or two, that will at least give you every chance you'll need to have at least one wholesome and rewarding relationship in your life.

A Dog's sense of time is quite different to ours. To them the only time that ever matters is right now. So unlike a young human, it's not going to take you fifteen years to find out that you did everything wrong.

With a Dog, it won't be fifteen seconds before they'll have let you know that you've slipped off the winner's pedestal.

At the beginning of your rehabilitation by canine, the little reminders from your beloved life coach might at times come a bit thick and fast, but then maybe they should, as what you are learning is after all a new language. I'm painfully aware that after forty thousand years of cohabitation this shouldn't be a new language for any human to have to learn, proof if any was needed that not all advancements can be heralded as progress.

However, please do not look at this possible barrage of reminders by your mate as an attack on your personality or anything negative towards you as a person, because the very last thing your life coach will want to do is make anyone feel any worse about themselves.

They don't want you to be any more self-conscious about who and what you are than you already are. They only want to make you more self-aware of how you are being, how you are acting and what sort of a person that instantly makes you out to be in the eyes of a Dog.

One saving grace, or at least something that you can at last, guarantee to have working on your side whenever you are dealing with Dogs, is their relentless determination to share their life changing capacity to forgive, take stock and move on, with you.

Living in the past is never going to do you any favours whenever you are around the guys who are only interested in what's going on right now. History is history to a Dog, to them, who you were yesterday means nothing compared to who you are being right now.

Although living with a life coach means you having to be under constant canine scrutiny, their ability to forgive and move on does at least give us all the chance of every day being a new day, a blank canvas, a fresh start or a new opportunity for you to shine and get through that day without allowing yourself to feel bad about yourself or letting the world in enough to ruin your day.

Demanding that the world stop biting you in order

to maintain your canine hero status will doubtless take many of us straight to the very heart of rehabilitation by canine, the roller coaster itself, where we begin to find out that so much of what we have been taught through our lives has been sold to us as a big, fat, ugly and detrimental pork pie.

The cold reality wakeup call comes knocking loud and clear when you realise that for a top Dog, being strong is no more a virtue than being able to eat or drink too much. Being strong is in fact a cancer of the mind, and is far from being a virtue of the free at all. It can only be a virtue for sheep, hamsters, the lost, the unworthy and poor souls who have absolutely no other choice than to continue being strong.

So, unless you are in prison or you have somebody constantly holding a gun against your head, you do indeed have a choice, and it's a choice you'll need to make quick, because on the road to being rehabilitated by a canine, you can forget all about demeaning yourself anymore by having to be strong.

Canines have a habit of occasionally demanding and bringing out a little more from us than just acting like a lobotomised drone, and this is where the emotional fun really shifts up a gear, and where you'll eventually get a much better chance of meeting the real you.

The most complicated thing about what you are about to do is getting your head around just how simple it is. Yes, your heart will race at times and doubts will do their very best to drown you, but all you have to do to kickstart this wonderful journey, is go into the depths of your emotional survival tool kit, find the word strong, tear it up, throw it away, and simply replace it with the word *brave*.

There are two very powerful and clear incentives for being brave rather than continuing to knuckle down and always be so strong.

The first is that being brave negates the need to be strong in the first place, and as being strong is likely only ever be a negative and reward free situation for anyone to find themselves in, why do you need to be good at it?

The second is something quite beautiful to witness and also something that will undoubtedly cross your path whilst you're searching on your canine journey, or to be more accurate, something that can hit some like a freight train, because this little nugget is the undoing of a simple truth, about fear.

When you are trying to suppress that fear of yours, again, just remember that nobody ever became addicted to being strong, and the chances of you loving yourself for always being strong will be hopelessly out gunned by how good you, and your Dog are going to start feeling about you, once being brave instead of always being strong becomes your new mantra.

For a wannabe canine hero, the days of you being a spectator of your own life must come to an end. The person holding the steering wheel and driving your life in the direction that you yourself want it to go, must, and can only ever be, you.

If, however, you're not absolutely sure who the real you actually is yet, please don't worry, because with your life coach by your side and it now getting harder and harder for you to keep saying yes when you really want to say no, the chances are that we are indeed, all about to find out who you really are.

So congratulations, my friend, you've taken the responsible, honourable, informed and well considered life choice of inviting a Dog into your life. In the interests of everybody getting the very best out of our human canine relationships, welcome to picking up poo, walking in the rain, vet bills, dog hair, forever saying 'what's that in your mouth' and constantly being forced to look at crazy things like the modern world, your life and indeed yourself, from a canine's perspective.

You will have to make adjustments, as not everything about owning a Dog is always going to fit absolutely perfectly into your current harmonious, well-adjusted, happy, grounded and rewarding life, but then for some of us, that is absolutely the whole point.

Whoever you are, and regardless of your background, the personal rewards for taking this road are always going to be in the very journey itself.

Accountants might be quick to point out the financial implications that come along with Dog ownership, but they'll always do so without ever considering the much higher price many of us can end up paying, if we don't in fact have somebody there constantly in our life keeping an eye on us.

If you're not familiar with Dog ownership, the thought of suddenly having to take precious time out of your busy life schedule to walk an animal on a regular basis, might seem like committing yourself to a life of drudgery and inconvenience.

A commitment, make no mistake, it most definitely is, even if one day you might just end up seeing it as the sort of commitment that you actually owed yourself.

A living, breathing, agenda free antidote to modern life, acting like your own personal, unbiased barometer, there every second of every day, letting you know whenever you happen to be acting like an idiot again.

To enjoy the full benefits of the drudgery of being able to walk your Dog properly, no matter how low you feel about yourself, however wound up, stressed out, angry, anxious or emotional the day might have got you, to stop things going from bad to worse, clicking that lead onto your best mate's collar just before you go off for that walk together, is when everything else in your crazy head must stop.

However inconvenient you might find having to keep pressing your emotions' reset button all the time. as you are aware, a Dog's unconditional love comes with one or two deal breaking caveats all by itself, and these terms and conditions for human canine harmony are never likely to come in to play more than when you are out walking in the big wide world with your life coach.

Walking with their owner is always going to mean so much more to a Dog than just being a simple form of exercise.

No amount of treats, toys, baby voices, cuddles, hugs or kisses will ever get you bonding as deeply or as quickly with a Dog as when you walk them.

Even if your garden is big enough for your Dog to run around like an idiot all day exhausting itself, the opportunity to bond with their owner on a primal level, simply by following their leader, at peace, journeying out in the world together on their walk.

For the animal that is Dog, and the animal that is the old hunter gatherer within each and every one of us, now caught up in today's plastic, clock watching, pill popping, stressed out, anxious, depressed and messed up world, our forty thousand years old friendship must surely be as valuable to us today as it ever has ever been?

Chapter Six
Rehabilitation by Canine

One Day however, I will step out of the dark
and I'll find myself free,
ready and able to live my own life,
content and soulfully at peace,
just being me.

As you earn your stripes on the road to becoming a canine hero, the relevance of the 'One Day' introduction to this book, if not already apparent, will begin to reveal itself.

Key points in this transition come after recognising that "oh, look at what my crazy dog does," usually means 'oh, look at what that crazy owner allows their dog to do.'

In just the same way as there is no such thing as dogs that pull on a lead whilst walking them, only dog owners who don't understand dogs, most crucially of all to a hunter gatherer caught up in the twenty-first century, dogs never take a day off from being dogs either.

Essentially, the big change comes when you stop allowing yourself to be a passenger or spectator in your own life, and start demanding things go your way instead of just hoping that everything turns out nice for you, not allowing everybody to be more important than you and facing what is probably a fear within if not all, then most people: the fear of not being loved.

Being brave instead of strong has little to do with wearing capes or suits of armour, but you still may well end up facing a demon or two or four, teen, hundred, depending who you are, but a lot of these demons will have originated from the same place.

A place that is irrelevant and no longer exists or even matters by the way, because if you look at the clock, you will notice that the time is exactly now, not then, nor is it tomorrow. This is today, my friend, exactly right at this moment, and more importantly for you at this very moment in time, is the fact that you have one end of a dog lead in one hand that has a perfectly tuned in lie detector waiting patiently at the other end of it.

If you are at all in any way anxious about the possibility of you losing out on love and affection with your dog, because you decided to take up the hero role instead of just trying to be your dog's buddy, you should know that as I'm writing this I am unable to sit properly in my own chair, in fact I'm all but sat on the edge of my seat.

Over the past ten months or so, I've often found myself sat like this, especially in the evenings, and no, not in the traditional 'edge of your seat' kind of way either, but in a French Bulldog called Bob kind of way.

Bob is what some people might call a rescue dog. I, however, just call him Bob, partly because I could never remember his old name, but mostly because I felt it best to give this little guy a fresh start in his new life, a complete disassociation from the past. Which is why he doesn't need to be tagged with the irrelevant, over used and often quite detrimental label of forever being called a rescue dog.

He's not a rescue anything, he's a dog, pure and simple.

It wasn't his fault that his previous owners didn't respect him for who he was, that they were too selfish and lazy with their own love, having never once taken the time to understand his needs as an animal, let alone fulfil any of them.

Ultimately, I met Bob because of his tenacious willingness to, at any given chance, bolt from the house whenever a door was open, which is when the fun for his then owners really began.

The constantly having to chase after a determined full of energy little dog, with zero recall, who darts around in manoeuvres that would surely even outsmart a Cheetah, was the breaking point in their relationship, and why Mr Ears ended up here, now once again wedged in tightly between the back of my chair and me, snoring his head off, as usual.

If he wakes up and needs to go outside, I'll turn the light on for him, open the door, let him out, close the door behind him and then carry on with what I was doing.

Even though he can walk right under the five bar gate to the outside world and the fence to the field that backs onto us here, is anything but dog proof.

Before you know it he'll be back, standing on his hind legs doing his 'let me in stance' front paws stretched out as high and wide as they'll go, tapping and scratching impatiently at the glass of the door.

Which is something I know his previous owners might find hard to believe, because the dog they knew and gave up on was a pain in the neck escape artist, that only seemed happy when giving his owners the run-around.

Which he was, very happy in fact, because what neither of them understood was that as much as Bob loves his food, and as much as he genuinely loves his affection, Bob's absolute favourite game of all, is being chased.

So, without dog treats or dog training, and no intention of me ever chasing after a dog, how has Mr Ears turned from the high energy runaway escape artist, into my shadow?

Chapter Seven
Mr Ears

To the couple who had originally bought him as a Pup, Bob, then just shy of a year old, had become hard work, and was now the cause of a lot of stress within their family home, and yet Bob's current owner can't talk about him without breaking into smile.

By following Bob's short journey from when I first met him to how he is today, I hope to outline and explain some of the basic but crucial points of what it took for me to win the heart and mind of a dog like Bob.

When I first met Bob it was soon patently obvious why his owners were finding him such hard work. David and Sarah, a young married couple, had a lot of love to give Bob, a lot of time for giving affection to him, lots of toys, bags of treats, a nice, posh, slightly chewed bed, leads and various different types of harnesses.

An array of different shampoos, food bowl, water bowl, travelling harness, crate, different types of grooming brushes, reams of paperwork, veterinary details, certificates, Puppy photos, even pictures of Bob's parents, a soft blanket and still absolutely no idea that Bob was in fact, a dog.

Bob may look a bit like an animal that has been hit in the face with a shovel, but to Sarah and David he had always been their baby. Whether you see them as cute or not, humanising a dog is a mistake no canine hero would ever think of making.

Yes, we all talk to our dogs, even if we know that they haven't got a clue as to what we're actually jabbering on about, but not respecting the fact that your baby's DNA is more than 99.7% Grey Wolf, is unlikely ever to work out very well for anyone.

Reality was that Bob lived in a playground with his two buddies, who loved him being the way he was. So much so that they'd often just randomly open the front door so they could all then go off and play Bob's favourite game, of being chased.

It didn't matter if they were just about to sit down for their meal, just about to watch their favourite TV programme or had something much better to do, nothing was ever too much trouble if it meant satisfying young Bob's excitable needs.

In human terms, at just shy of a year old, Bob was then the equivalent of a young teenage lad, who had lived his whole life without responsibility, structure or leadership.

Which makes it hard then when you have only just met, to make an accurate assessment as to what kind of a dog you are actually looking at, by that I mostly mean what kind of temperament they are.

His love of running around so much, however, told

me that he was a physically healthy dog, and the fact that the excitable little fellow was now sleeping at my feet as I talked with Sarah and David about him, told me all I really needed to know.

Giving up a dog, even if that relationship hasn't necessarily been all that harmonious, isn't always the easiest thing in the world to do. Bob falling asleep at my feet like that after I'd been ignoring him for so long, was however probably the most reassuring thing for Sarah and David to see too, even if they hadn't fully understood exactly what Bob was clearly telling me by doing so.

From the very moment I arrived at their home, Bob had done his level best to try and get my attention, darting around like a rat on the Titanic, jumping up and over everything, bouncing around on the furniture, gruffing and barking at me, doing just about everything he could to get me to engage in any sort of game with him.

Even though, to his obvious and escalating frustration, I continued to completely ignore Bob, of course, the very last thing I was actually doing was ignoring him.

But this was our first meeting after all, and I knew that if I didn't want Bob to see me as just another one of his playmates or another idiot to chase him around all day, I'd have to be and act in a completely different way to Sarah and David.

By ignoring his funny but unwanted, over excitable

and persistent behaviour, I was sending out a loud and clear message to young Bob, and well he knew it.

As super cute as he undoubtedly is, and as much fun as he is to be around, Bob, from now on, was going to have to earn every little bit of attention or affection he'd get from his new owner. His free ride was over. This tail was no longer going to be wagging the dog.

After about half an hour or so I was signing Bob's paperwork to take ownership of him, much to my own delight and the gob-smacked bemusement of both Sarah and David. By that time Mr Ears had given up on all of his riotous showboating and thrown in the towel, deciding to then instead lay down and go to sleep, but not in his own bed or on the sofa, but at my feet, even though by then I still hadn't even so much as made eye contact with him yet.

After he'd been laying there for a few minutes, I leaned down, and slowly massaged his back for him whilst he laid on his side. He raised his head and looked back over his shoulder at me, and that was when I first made eye contact with him.

My message by then was as clear to him as his had been to me by him lying there at my feet in the first place.

What I meant by earning me, was that from now on, to get anything from me at all — his food, being given affection, his tennis ball through to being allowed to go outside by himself — Bob would always have to give me something first, and it was something Mr Ears wasn't overly used to giving anybody.

So far little Bob had absolutely no reason not to trust me, and every reason to respect me, and I personally will do all I can through our life together to make sure those parameters for him will never change.

By taking the canine hero stance with him right from the get-go, I still got to see how cute he was, how much fun he could be, but I also then got to see his true colours, and more importantly to me, just how ready he was for calm leadership in his life, without me once ever having to try to buy his affection or worrying whether he liked me or not.

The depth of bond and love that you will receive back from a dog, by you taking up the canine hero roll, will far outweigh the superficial, see-through, plastic love you'll only ever experience by wanting to be their friend.

Bottom line is, at least for a thick skinned, stone hearted, emotionless, dog hating guy like me, is why would I waste any of my time and energy wanting to be liked by dogs when I know for a lot less effort I can be adored?

There were three people in that room. Two of them had spent the best part of a year gushing their humanised love and affection all over their baby, Bob, but the reward for their efforts and eventual heartbreak was seeing him calmly asleep at the feet of a bloke that hadn't even acknowledged him yet.

But with young Sarah and David now as reassured about Bob's future happiness, as I myself was ever likely to make them at that time, and Mr Ears himself already in a calm, follower state of mind, it was time for us to up stumps and head for home.

The rewards for living in the now were then further sledgehammered home for Sarah and David as they watched the two of us walk off together. Little Bob had absolutely no idea where he was going or how long he was going for, and clearly didn't care. He knew nothing about my history, and I didn't care about his. To him, all that mattered was that this new guy and he were now on an adventure, going somewhere, walking together, in unison, as one, and right at that moment, that was absolutely all Bob was focused on and indeed all he cared about.

But then that's the canine mind for you. In the same way that dogs don't have the mental capacity to be able to rationalise, they don't do guilt either. Unlike humans, dogs don't willingly or possessively drag the past around with them. To a dog, right now is always as good a time as there'll ever be to move on and make the most of life.

Which brings us to what probably has to be the most important conversation anyone can ever have with a canine.

Between leaving Sarah and David's place and Bob's new home, was the opportunity for us both to get to know each other on a primal level, where the foundations to a human canine relationship are built, where slates get cleaned and reset buttons get pushed.

I am of course, talking about the walk.

Chapter Eight
Baby Steps

From naive over babying to outright conscious abuse, it can be very easy for an otherwise would have been well behaved dog to become problematical for their owners, and to then also go on to be written off by the rest of the world as a no hoper, or special needs simply because they have never been understood and respected for being who or what they are.

Spoilt to death as a human baby maybe, but rewarded and fulfilled as a dog? No manners or respect? Disruptive and destructive? Uncontrollable? High Energy?

Little Bob and his previous owners were caught up in a no win, catch twenty-two situation. Because they had left themselves with little confidence and almost no control over their baby, it meant a frustrated, young, full of energy dog, with absolutely no structure in his life, who didn't even get to be walked regularly.

Which all too often meant Bob was then left with nowhere to expend his boundless frustrated youthful energy, other than within the confines of 'his' home, hence his incessant demands, treating the home as a playground, along with his love of escaping and then being chased.

Up until now, the only time Bob had ever really experienced being calm, was when he was asleep, which more often than not was only after 'he' had worn 'himself' out, but once again, this was something that was about to change.

The walk that little Bob and I were now enjoying together, had begun the very moment that I made eye contact with him back in his old home.

He was calm, and laying on his side with his back to me, and a dog sat or laying close by with their back to you, is that dog telling you in no uncertain terms that they not only like you enough to want to be in your company, but giving you their back means they also trust you completely too. Me giving Bob affection at that time, along with my eye contact, when he was behaving exactly how I wanted him to be, was the reward and endorsement that he had been looking for.

From that point on Bob then understood exactly how to get my attention, the attention that so far, despite all his previous catalogue of efforts, he'd not been able to attract ever since I'd arrived at Sarah and David's. He would quickly learn that excited dogs never get fed in his new home, and that the quickest way for him to get anything he wanted, was to give me a calm state of mind first.

The calm state of mind I'm talking about, is absolutely where every dog walk should really always start, and by that, I am not just talking about the dog.

Whenever you meet a new dog, it is always better to understand the situation they are in from a canine perspective, than be judgemental of it from an emotional stand point. Whether you've just met in a loving home of an out of depth couple like Sarah and David, or within the public no-go zones of dog pounds and rescue centres, the rules are always the same.

Cute, funny as hell, pocket-sized dog or sixty kilos full of fear and ready to rip your face off, if you go anywhere near them, dogs are dogs, and they all speak the same language.

If you are going to be the first human being that a dog has ever been able to have any belief in, you will no doubt have just earned yourself a shadow, but you'll be unlikely ever to do this if all you bring to the party is a humanised over excitable, sentimental, emotionally driven imagination.

By making little Bob earn any of my attention or affection I wasn't denying him love, nor was I bringing his fun life to an end. In reality, I was doing anything but.

As he happily walked away from Sarah and David's by my side, he had no idea that being chased until he was exhausted was going to be a regular part of his daily routine or that he'd still be the cheeky dog stuck in play mode initiating the games, even if it wasn't going to be me doing any of the chasing.

Fast forward to today and Bob knows full well that if he runs away from me, I'll just turn and walk away in the opposite direction, and then wait for him to come and chase after me. Yes, I know that might be a heart in mouth, leap of faith for some people to take, but then why would a dog run away from the thing he loves the most?

It can be easy to get frustrated at people like Sarah and David, when you see so much potential fulfilment and happiness fail comprehensively, simply because of a lack of understanding of dogs by their owners. In just the same way it can be all but impossible not to get emotional at places like rescue centres, and feel sorry for the guys stuck in the cages there, but you're unlikely to be doing yourself or them many favours if you ever let their environment get the better of you.

They may have been stuck there forever but dogs have no idea what a dog pound or rescue centre is. They don't know that they're not meant to be there or that they could be having a much better life somewhere else as somebody's life coach. To a dog it's just today, we are here and that's the way it is, but what will matter to that dog right at that moment is you, how you are being, how you are acting, and how they then see you.

This is when the ball will be firmly in your court, whether that dog is then set to continue being the high energy, uncontrollable, destructive, disruptive, disrespectful little dog with no manners, that ultimately was given up on or whether you are you ready to start demanding, instead of just hoping things turn out nice for you, win his heart and mind, introduce some fundamental balance into his life and make sure that he'll never be given up on again?

It is beyond unfair to write a dog off as problematic if they have never been respected as a dog or if the only structure in their life so far has been canine chaos.

The reality is that although Bob maybe a dog stuck in permanent play mode, he is far from being a high energy needy dog that is always in your face or constantly on the go at all, and he doesn't have to be walked ten thousand miles every day to keep him that way either.

A chaotic home, a fundamental lack of leadership qualities and utter contempt for the canine mind had led both Sarah and David on a merry dance whenever they tried to walk Bob. As soon as either of them went anywhere near a dog lead, Bob's turbo would instantly kick in and he'd be away, shooting off the excitement scale from ever ready to berserk in all but seconds, with Sarah's anxiety, doubts and dread then racing away doing exactly the same thing.

Even before the front door was open we had an over excited dog ready to go out and have fun in his world but with an owner full of dread, already seeing in her mind's eye what was about to happen. Expecting the pulling, the challenging cars as they drove by, needing to sniff here, needing to sniff there, crossing over back and forth in front of her like a hover mower, with no interest in Sarah at all but plenty of interest, energy and time to meet or try to get to any other dogs or anybody else that he saw out on his travels.

But then that is what can happen when you allow your dog to take you for a walk.

This is why I said that our walk began the moment I made eye contact with him. At that time he was calm, and had already submitted to both me and the situation, handing me the perfect state of mind to then be able take my dog out on my walk.

My head wasn't full of anxiety or dread of what might be about to happen, I wasn't foreseeing me being pulled or dragged anywhere any time soon by Mr Ears, nor was I seeing him chasing after cars or trying to get to other dogs, and unlike Sarah, I couldn't wait to be walking him.

But, with this being our first meeting and first ever walk together, I had all the time in the world to do this right. Calm respectful dogs don't bite, chase, pull or run away, and Bob laying at my feet was already calm, so all I had to do from then on was make sure he stayed that way.

Bob seeing the front door open, up until this point in his life had always meant, I'm out of here, game on everybody, chase me, his green light for him to scarper and have some fun.

But as we said goodbye to Sarah and David young Bob just sat there looking out, calmly sniffing the air, waiting, no intention of running anywhere. Had he tried to, all I would have done is either block him or stop him by using his lead, have him sit back down again until he had lost interest in what 'he' wanted to do, and had given that calm follower state of mind back to me again.

When a police dog handler releases a dog into a house to track down criminals, the dog always goes in first, through that doorway first, that entrance first, the gateway in to somewhere new, first. Because he came in first, PC Shepherd has automatically then become the master of that zone, he's the one in charge of that place, and he's been let in there in an excited and determined to please state of mind.

However, if there are no baddies in there for him to bring down, the next problem for the police officers involved can be making sure PC Shepherd knows that his job is already done.

As any dog will see it, because the dog went through that doorway first and was encouraged to do so by the handler following him, the dog instantly became the boss, whilst in a dominant and excited state of mind.

Which is the absolute opposite of what we as a canine hero want to achieve before we set off out on our walks. A calm state of mind, combined with each of you knowing exactly who is leading and who is following, are two huge steps in anyone wanting to avoid having their arm pulled out of its socket by the very dog they themselves might have just set to task, just like PC Shepherd had been.

These basic points may sound silly, inconvenient or even insignificant to us, but to a dog it can mean a great deal, and if we don't notice or appreciate how dogs think, we can end up not only confusing the hell out of our life coach, but we can also be unwittingly setting ourselves up to fail or at least setting ourselves up for a walk that nobody really enjoys.

To highlight the importance of these maybe silly, inconvenient, or insignificant points, imagine taking Mr Ears out of this doorway scenario for a minute, and replacing him instead with a few dogs. A pack, half a dozen Huskies say, and not only Huskies but Huskies that for some reason best known to their owner are also wearing harnesses, but then as Huskies, harnesses and being very happy to drag something behind them for miles and miles every day they should do the trick nicely. If not Huskies, then what about a few Pitbull Terriers, dogs capable of dragging something up to thirty times heavier than their own body weight.

Stoke this fire by saying none of the dogs looking at you right now have been walked for a few days, they are healthy, fit and keen to get going. You happen to be holding their dog leads, and this, by the way, also happens to be the very first time you guys have been introduced to each other.

So, how focused are we now, and what kind of mind set are we tapping into for these guys, and is that mindset in any way at all different to how we were with little Bob?

Are we going to be rewarding excitable dominant behaviour anytime soon or are we going to keep our cool and demand everybody behaves themselves?

Who is setting the pace in the room right now, you or them, and are we ourselves calm enough to enable the dogs to be calm at all?

As we then open the door to the outside world, have we made sure everybody in the room knows exactly who is running the show and who is going to be leading the way on this particular walk, or have your impatience, doubts, low expectations, excitement or your fears already set you up to be hanging on to the back of a runaway train again?

The choice will have been all yours, not theirs.

To dogs it won't matter why you are acting the way you are, they'll just accept that this is how you are and will then instantly react accordingly. In just the same way it wasn't little Bob's fault that Sarah allowed him to be so disruptive all the time.

You allow it, you make it happen, and then you blame the dog for it, nobody learns anything and nobody involved gets to win, isn't that right, Sarah.

Bob's story is as good as any for this book to have begun with the 'One Day' introduction. As with all dogs, Bob came pre-packaged with his own personal message that sadly, a modern day emotional stress head was too busy Larkin about to hear.

Not recognising or respecting him as a dog made it impossible for Sarah to see young Bob as any kind of life coach, even though he was desperately trying to hand her life tools that would not only better prepare her for him, her first 'baby', but without question would help her in the future through the joys of actual motherhood, and beyond.

He may be a cheeky little fellow and he may well spend most of his waking hours stuck in play mode, but if Sarah had really wanted to understand what ground zero relaxation was, if she had wanted to have access to the reset button that would stop crazy always running away with her day. If she had really wanted the ability to click her fingers and instantly take back control, make everything stop, to put everything down, demanding to have things go her way and then soak up the benefits of living in the moment, if she had read the 'One Day' introduction to this book and thought one day that will be me, she maybe shouldn't have just let the perfect life coach for her walk happily out of the door, with me.

Chapter Nine
Missed Opportunity

Identifying why Bob was acting as unruly as he was when I first met him, took no more than a few seconds of actually meeting with Sarah. In truth, and only because this sort of problem is sadly not that uncommon, I already had a pretty good idea of where the blame was likely to lay regarding Bob's unwanted behaviour, long before we'd actually met.

Then seeing Mr Ears doing his party piece, but more importantly, seeing how big softy, nurturing mummy, Sarah, the ever-loving spectator, was reacting to Bob doing his party piece, only confirmed what I already suspected.

For the most part, Bob's very simple requirements for 'his' rehabilitation were all but done and dusted before I had even taken ownership of him, as he'd gone from berserk to butter wouldn't melt in his mouth just by me ignoring him.

I know deep down both Sarah and David struggled a bit with this, seeing the dog they thought they knew being all calm and goody two shoes for me. It was something of a shock to them, how somebody Bob didn't even know could just breeze into crazy and put a fire out without actually doing anything.

Painful reality for some people maybe, but there is absolutely no mystery as to how I was able to win little Bob over so easily that day. Sarah may well have seen me as some kind of Dr Doolittle at the time but I'm not, nor have I ever been. In fact I'm just like Sarah herself, in that the only natural born abilities I may ever have been blessed with regarding dogs, was that from birth I have always loved them.

Sarah and I may not look anything like each other, but as far as Bob was concerned the only difference that really mattered to him at all, was how different we acted towards him.

The human population of Britain has not doubled since 1990, neither has the number of dogs we have here, yet a generation after banning certain 'aggressive' breeds and the introduction of the 1991 Dangerous Dogs Act, the problem of dog bites is now statistically twice as bad today as it was back in 1990.

In Britain, there is roughly the equivalent of one Dog per every seven human beings — working dogs, trackers, search and rescue, hunting dogs, therapy dogs, medical detection, service and protection dogs, sniffers, guards, guides, pets and companions.

Dogs were already a big part of our daily lives long before civilisation had even begun. Today there are about ten million dogs amongst us in Britain, and it is unlikely they'll be disappearing out of our lives any time soon.

From way back in the Ice Age, through the plastic present and for the rest of time, it will never be the dog's fault if the largest brain on the planet happens to have been too busy Larkin about to remember exactly who they are.

Having a life coach suddenly turn up in her life was the last thing Sarah was ready for when she bought little Bob. She was only really interested in buying into the dream of owning a pet, a teddy bear, a cute looking guy that would be good company for her, fun to be around with lots of cuddles and endless amounts of happy times spent together. But instead she ended up with Bob, an animal that came with his own mind and own instinctive needs, that sadly for them both, were rarely ever met.

The pet Sarah had longed for, against the dog Sarah eventually ended up with, soon became two very different things, whereas what I had demanded from Bob from the very beginning, I got straight away, and not only that but he continues to freely give it to me on an everyday basis.

Ultimately my reward for playing the canine hero card instead of just being a canine doormat, is that I'm now the proud and lucky owner of a very special, impossibly cute and constantly funny little dog, that adores me about as much as I adore him.

He's great company and fun to be around, and although he may only be small in stature, I know he'd already leave a huge hole behind him if he was no longer here.

Furthermore, I have absolutely no doubt in my mind that he is, and always was, exactly the dog Sarah herself had in fact always dreamed of owning.

Not recognising or respecting Mr Ears for what he is, meant Sarah not only missed out on a wonderful relationship with what should have been the perfect dog for her, but in turning her back on Bob, I will argue to anybody that she also unwittingly gave up on herself too.

The six out of seven people in Britain who will never actually own a dog, may not necessarily see any value in everyone being taught the basics of canine psychology and protocol through our school years.

Even though it would without question go a lot further than the 1991 Dangerous Dogs Act ever has or ever could go, in helping prevent hundreds of people needlessly getting themselves bitten or attacked by dogs every day.

Like it or not, the reality is that whoever you happen to be, we are all of us nature before we are anything else, and it therefore should not come as a huge shock to anybody that balance and soulful happiness might actually be found in acknowledging, understanding and respecting the very thing that we all are.

This simple reconnection with our closest link with nature, would undoubtedly help prevent the likes of young Sarah blindly missing out on the life changing opportunity of having a rewarding and harmonious relationship with a life coach called Bob, a little guy that was doing all he could to convince her to grab a hold of her own life for the sake of herself, and be the Sarah that he could then naturally look up to and adore.

If you've become too good at allowing a highly strung negative imagination, your anger, your frustration, your doubts, your fears, your anxiety or your low self-worth to continually run away and take over your day, then it is probably best that you don't get a dog like Bob.

If you have no intention of ever taking responsibility for how you allow yourself act and feel or are happy to just continue being crazy, don't get a dog like Bob.

If you think being a victim is an acceptable way of life or think anyone else is more important than you, then please don't get a dog like Bob.

If you think you can buy love with plastic treats or believe rehabilitating a canine is all about training the dog, don't get a dog like Bob.

If you think denial is your friend or you find yourself constantly saying yes when you really want to say no, you'd be quite mad to get yourself a dog like Bob.

If you wish that you were somebody else or think you are smarter and more advanced than our ancestors were, definitely don't get a dog like Bob.

If you think being a doormat is an endearing foundation for love to grow on, never, ever, ever, get a dog like Bob.

However, if you're tired of being dragged around by life, think it might be time for you to start believing in yourself a bit more, and are interested in taking back some of the control that you may never have actually had, but need a friend to help you get there.

If you are sick of being a doormat and want to claim the walk through life that is rightfully yours, if you finally and genuinely no longer care what others think of you, If you have the courage to put the love and wellbeing of your best mate before your own doubts and insecurities.

If for some reason you actually need an incentive to step off the hamster wheel every now and again, to clear the mist, take a time out to touch base with you, to stop the clock, to catch your breath, making sure that you're not just once again nose down running in the wrong direction.

If you feel it might be time for you to step out of the shadows of your own life, and learn how to be the best version of you that you yourself have ever known. If you need somebody to teach you the real meaning of time, someone who will always steer you back onto your path if you happen to lose your way again or if you'd like a mate who just simply needs you to be a hero, then yes, it is probably time that you did yourself and everyone around you a big favour, and went out and got yourself a dog, absolutely one hundred percent just like Bob.

Chapter Ten
Old Dogs, New Tricks

This chapter is the new chapter in your life that only you yourself can write.

Having stepped up and won their hearts and minds, you will have no doubt listened to the one mother that each and every one of us should actually listen to, and in doing so, you will no doubt have found a certain peace within you too.

That peace belongs to you, my friend, and should have always been yours. It is your strength, and the reason you now have a Dog in your life, is to make sure you learn how to never to give that peace of you away, ever again.

Chapter Eleven
Stuff

The brightest star in our night sky is Sirius, officially known as Alpha Canis Majoris, or more commonly known as the Dog Star.

A Dog can smell something up to forty feet underground.

A Dog can hear four times further than we can.

A Dog can smell your emotions.

The pattern on a Dog's nose is as unique as a human fingerprint.

Something to remember next time you are walking your dog along roads or paths on a hot summer day, Dogs sweat through their paws.

When Dogs make eye contact with a human being, they will always look into our right eye first. Their focus will initially concentrate on our right eye, almost ignoring our left eyes completely, just as we humans do with each other. Dogs don't do this when looking at each other or with any other animal, just us, only because it is a human trait that we all do with each other and dogs have noticed this, even if you yourself hadn't.

Dogs see colours differently to us. Our eyes see with yellow, blue and red — Dogs only have yellow and blue. Hence why they can struggle sometimes to see something like a tennis ball on grass, obvious to us maybe, but it can be hiding in plain sight for a Dog. In fact if it isn't moving, a tennis ball is often found using scent rather than by sight. but then born deaf and blind, to Dog, using their nose is their primary sense. We have to see something before we believe it, but you'll never fool a Dog's nose.

Printed in Great Britain
by Amazon

13299741R00050